12 REASONS YOU SHOULD SMASH YOUR CELL PHONE

Bowen Craig
with Kelly Codling

12 REASONS YOU SHOULD **SMASH** YOUR **CELL PHONE**

ISBN 979-8-9997899-0-7

Published in the United States of America by
Bilbo Books Publishing

www.BilboBooks.com
bilbobookspublishing@gmail.com
(706)-549-1597
Athens, Georgia

12 REASONS YOU SHOULD SMASH YOUR CELL PHONE

Fifteen years ago or so I read the funniest, weirdest, saddest, most thought-provoking, news story ever written. It was about the city fathers of Vienna, Austria having to coat their electricity poles in bubble wrap…in order to keep teenagers from running into them.

Sure, teenagers have always been stupid, but now they're so mind-blowingly stupid that they're just running headlong into giant metal poles? Was there another factor in Austria's Dumb Teenager trend, a factor other than hormones or lazy, permissive Euro-parenting? Perhaps a pocket-sized, rectangular, flashing idiot box? It turns out that Austrian teenagers were too busy looking at their cell phones to even notice the stationary, large, looming metallic obstacle in their path, and this was happening so often that the city felt the need to do something about it.

Cell phones ruin everything.

Cell phones are evil.

True evil tricks us into thinking it's good.

This stupidity, though worldwide, is of course, magnified in America. If there's a dumb trend out there, we're going to corner the market on it. It's just what we do.

Is there a sadder sight in modern America than a nuclear family of four sitting around a restaurant dinner table and NOT talking to each other for an hour-and-a-half? A curious and well-meaning time traveling visitor from any point from the beginning of human history until a few years after 2000 A.D. might understandably assume that they were all deaf and mad at each other, or that they were a family of wandering monks each having recently taken a vow of silence, or that they were all just brain-dead wastes of human potential. Our time traveler would be wrong if he guessed A or B, but completely and totally correct if he guessed C. Yes, they're all brain-dead automatons just going through the motions of life, not coming anywhere close to actually living. And why? Because of the soul-sucking plastic rectangular pocket gods they call cell-phones.

Cell phones are the most dangerous, most evil, most damaging inventions ever. Unlike, say, napalm, nuclear bombs, or Austrian teenagers, which we can all agree are pretty damn evil, the reason cell phones aren't generally put in that category of undeniable evil is that most people don't seem to consciously even realize that this little electronic pile of nonsense through which they've organized their entire lives is indeed the worst thing they've ever bought, and is currently sucking them down into a pit of anger and social control. Can they turn their lives around? Can they get off the unquestioning zombie moving sidewalk to pointlessness? Sure, of course they can. **And the first step is smashing the living shit out of their cell phones.**

In this book I will explore the massive amounts of dumbassery surrounding cell phones. With some mild help from (literally) the only other person I know who hates cell phones as much as I do, Jamaican restaurateur and philosopher Kelbourne "Kelly" Codling, we will look at twelve reasons you should smash your cell phone and free yourself from the invisible handcuffs these things slowly and subtly affix to your brain.

ACKNOWLEDGEMENTS

I'd like to thank Verizon, Sprint, AT&T and Apple for being horrible corporate citizens and the worst drug dealers in human history. Without you this book would not have been possible.

I'd like to thank the memory of Steve Jobs, and for the record, unlike everyone else, I think you were a slimy, short-sighted piece of monkey shit. Sorry to speak ill of the dead, but your legacy should by rights be closer to that of the guy who invented methamphetamine than to Nikola Tesla.

I'd also like to thank Kelly Codling, for always being right and for joining me as I write and philosophize.

Sarah Klipper - I've never met an artist/ technologist before who is actually both. Your design work is simply genius.

I'd like to thank my mother, Carey Bowen Craig, and my mentor, William Elrod "Roddy" Bray, for teaching me to question everything. It may not have led to my being a hit at dinner parties, but damn, it helps keep you out of the invisible handcuffs.

REASON #1 you should SMASH YOUR CELL PHONE:

*They are Dumbing you Down...
and by this point you're
probably too dumb to notice*

They just are. Deep down you *know* they are. I will happily admit that this particular reason for a good ole' cellular smashfest is a continuation of the slow-growing trend of 20th century electronics, all of which has collectively dumbed us down, usually too ploddingly and methodically for us to notice. The frog in the pan metaphor works here (for the record, it's a scientifically untrue and wildly overused analogy of the best way to boil a frog, as if that's useful information).

The radio may have started this trend, but radio is not nearly as guilty as its more visually-oriented children. Still, the miraculous invention of the radio was a small step for man and a giant step for the ancestors of the douchebags who now control us through flashing pocket rectangles.

Radio plays (or serials, or really any narrative radio storytelling) were a tiny step in the wrong direction. Compare them to actual stage plays. First off, to see a play you had to go out, to go to a theater, and you probably dressed up in your Sunday Best to do it. You had to watch and listen. You had to visualize the unseen props and offstage characters and between-scene plot points. In other words you had to pay more attention, and use your brain a little bit, especially if you wanted to have an intelligent conversation at Intermission. Since there were others around you, there was an inherent social aspect to the stage play, which didn't transfer entirely to the radio.

TV definitely dumbed us down even farther. This slow erosion of critical thinking began with the advent of the television. It was the most passive entertainment yet devised. All you needed was electricity and a couch and you could do absolutely nothing for days on end. The brain is a muscle, and muscles need exercise. Parents did notice that their children were slowly morphing into mindless drones, but only a handful of them did much of anything to correct the problem. Making their children sit a little farther away to watch their televisions was common, and good parents limited their children's screen time (an idea that has since all but evaporated from the parenting handbook, right when it was needed most).

And don't get me started on the Internet. Too late. I was alive for the early days of the internet. I remember its promise. I recall the pronouncement of future world harmony resulting from this unprecedented tool of "connection." Ooh, the irony now seems palpable, but at first the internet was heralded as a possible starting place for, if you can believe it, world peace. Now we run weapons system *through* the internet. Now we control bomber drones with wireless technology and murder people from the sky. Now the internet has divided America into rigid political camps, causing fights, hatred and a disorganized orgy of poorly-thought-out-opinions. Thanksgiving with the family already had enough arguments, but at least they used to involve actual thought-out personal political positions. Now both sides of this false equation are just repeating crap they read online, and probably both truly believe they're expressing original thought. The internet has become a giant lie.

But even that massive leap backwards would've been manageable if we just hadn't made it pocket-sized. Carrying this telephone/internet access point around with us has, as far as I can see, only one positive use. Although I hate cell phones to such an extent that I felt the need to write a book about how much I hate them, even I can recognize the one decent feature of the cell phone – emergency calls. I only admit this because it's good debate policy to grant the other side a few points. I'll give it one, and only one point. It is helpful in an emergency.

But it's not as if emergencies are new creations, other than those *caused by* the internet. We've been problem solving since the first caveman noticed that saber-toothed tiger loitering outside the mouth of his cave.

One thing cell phones are definitively not doing is improving our general intelligence. If the American education system were even slightly better we might come to obvious realization that allowing students their cell phones in school is simply asking for our national laziness level to increase by leaps and bounds. Sadly, we're now too dumb to realize how dumb we're getting.

Let's break this down a bit.

#1 — It's just so easy

The ease with which "information" can be found on cell phones makes us think of them partially as reference tools, and somehow since they're in our pockets we can easily make ourselves forget just how much information on the internet is complete and utter bullshit. This ease has, in and of itself, caused us to believe that internet inquiry is somehow merely a faster version of research methodologies of the past. But anyone who has spent time in a library, combing through old tomes or spinning microfilm or dusting off ancient books knows that ALL research is at least somewhat suspect. Why do you think real reporters (another unfortunately endangered species, thanks largely to internet-linked cell phones) require two reliable sources before going to print? Why do you think heavily-referenced research papers are so loaded with multiple citations and pages of footnotes or endnotes? It's because even eye-witness accounts are subject to our own personal quirks and biases. Ask a beat cop sometime how different two accounts of the same car crash are. Despite the cell phones' effort, we're still at least somewhat different than all other people, thank God.

And yet, people trust the results of pocket Google searches. It's a pay-to-play phone book/classified ad and still we seem to have almost godlike faith in its answers, even though, for now, most of us still know, down deep, how much of the internet is utter crap. The ease makes it so much simpler to do internet research instead of actual, go-to-the-source book-based research, even though the fact that one has to edit a book and doesn't have to check one's sources or fact check anything before posting online rarely enters our brains. Fact checking and the internet are like chunky peanut butter and whale sperm, they're not in the least bit related, and they should disgust us, much like chunky whale semen, and yet, they don't…possibly cell phones have dumbed us down to the point that we'd be willing to drink peanut-flavored whale sperm, if someone pretty and perky online told us that it has medicinal benefits.

It's not just the simplicity of it, it's also the fact that so much of modern education is internet-based that makes people think it's always the primary go-to for learning about anything. If that's what you did in first grade and in twelfth grade, it's more than likely what you'll do in college and beyond.

#2 – Retention, or the lack thereof

Studies have shown that we retain less of what we read online than in books. It's true. Studies have also shown that longhand writing of notes burns the information into the brain in a way that typing notes into a computer does not. I assume that one is like any other muscle memory. If you practice hitting a fastball or driving a car or plowing a field enough times, then you're going to remember how to do it when it counts. You're going to remember it without having to pull it up in your memory. They call that muscle memory, and the brain is a muscle.

Anything internet-related is temporary. We seem to think that there's no such thing as editing the internet, no such thing as search engine manipulation, even when we know down deep that there is. The "facts" are routinely manipulated online. Search engines don't freeze information. Somehow they've convinced us that they do, but since they run the internet's phone book, they have multiple methodologies for censorship, including simply boosting lies and pushing the truth farther down their list. The technologists who run search engines often have ulterior motives (mainly greed-related, but sometimes political in nature). Why do you think the results of searches aren't listed alphabetically, but instead are ranked in terms of their popularity? It's not to make us smarter.

#3 — It's easier than ever before for governments and companies to censor the truth

Online platforms' censorship activities on behalf of the worst aspects of the U.S. government during the Covid pandemic proves how much easier it is now to censor online information and control the flow of information/

propaganda than the arrangement of the internet would suggest. YouTube, the world's favorite video sharing/human shaming service, is still censoring a lot of data surrounding that dark bizarre period, and I'm writing this three years after everyone realized that those "vaccines" were at best placebos, at worst slow euthanasia. I won't dwell too long on this one, because that era was confusing enough. Also around half of the people I know are comforted by propaganda…the stupid half.

I'm aware that not everyone agrees with me about information weaponization about the "pandemic." A strange aspect of human nature is that we tend to believe BIG lies much more easily than the small ones. We don't believe that Sharon cheated on Brad with Steve, but we accept completely bullshit justifications for sending our children to go to war with a country we've never even heard of. Americans have been lied into almost every war we've ever fought. Weapons of mass destruction in Iraq, remembering *The*

Maine, the Gulf of Tonkin. Some say that we even had advance knowledge of Pearl Harbor, but since World War II was an understandable war, we ignore that one. I'm only using war as an example because the pocket-internet is undoubtedly going to try to propagandize us into another one soon enough, so we should be ready and realize that it probably won't be a saving-humanity-from-evil kind of war, like WWII.

Everything about the internet, especially the pocket-sized internet, is inherently temporary, and yet we don't consciously realize this when we use it as a reference tool. We see it as permanent.

KELLY SAYS:

In order for you to understand where I'm coming from, let me tell you that I took my publisher (Bo) and my photographer (Matt) with me to Jamaica to take pictures and get information about the way I grew up, about my family and the country. We went up in the country to talk to people I went to school with, people who knew my family and knew me when I was little.

My father was a farmer in Rock Springs, up in the interior mountains of Trelawny Province, in Jamaica. My father was a farmer. We grew yellow yams, coffee, sugarcane, bananas, pimento and other crops, depending on the season. Pimento comes in the summer, sugarcane from December to June. We had cows, goats, pigs, chickens and a variety of all of the other animals that live on farms.

Growing up on a farm is not easy. We had to get up early, really, really early, at 4 A.M., to feed the animals. Then I had to change and walk down the mountain a bit to go to school, then come back for lunch, then back to school, then back home for chores. I got to know that mountain well.

In this book Bo and I hope to show you that life was better before cell phones. Technology can be a good thing, but not always. Not even often these days.

One time technology *was* good was when my father finally bought a truck. Before the truck we had to lug a cart full of crops down the mountain to sell them at market. It would take 3 to 4 hours on foot, with the donkey hauling the cart doing some of the work. After my father bought the truck, it only took an hour and a half. That truck revolutionized our lives, changed them for the better. Everybody would pile their crops in the back and we'd go down to market together. That truck was the opposite of the cell phone. It didn't control our lives, didn't make us afraid of invisible nonsense, it just did what we needed it to do, and it helped.

REASON #2 you should SMASH YOUR CELL PHONE:

Your attention span is now so short that you can't finish a decent sent...

Everyone realizes this one, and yet no one seems particularly phased by it. Once more, the advent of twentieth century entertainment strikes us in an important spot. We need attention spans longer than crackhead kittens. In order to do anything at all worth doing, we need to be able to retain focus long enough to do it. This is not a grand revelation.

Instead of smashing the cell phones, which would eventually lead us to be able to collectively pay attention to one thing for more than seven straight seconds (and yes it really is *that* bad), we adjust the other side of the equation, the demand not the supply. We ought to increase the supply of attention, instead of demanding things that require shorter attention spans: home dinner delivery instead of cooking, shorter and shorter media to entertain us. And the internet, while it is the drug dealer, is more than willing to change the drug formula so that instead of 20 minute videos, we get 10 minutes. Instead of a 30 minute program, we get the catchy sounds bites, which we find where? You guessed it, on the internet. It's a snake chasing its tail. It's the world's slowest and longest suicide pact, and we're all mini-Neros, fiddling while Rome burns.

If only they hadn't shrunk it to fit in our pockets, we might still be sailing the waters of sanity, instead of drowning in the whirlpool of flashing idiocy.

It hasn't helped our collective laziness either. I'm not completely sold on the idea that technology inherently makes us lazier, but it's getting harder to deny the evidence with each passing day. You can now order dinner over the cell phone, to be delivered to your door. You can pay your damn taxes via cell phone now. (It's a terrible idea for multiple reasons, but it's still doable.) You can book vacations, check the weather report, and watch movies. This ease contributes not only to our shrinking attention spans, but they also make people think that this convenience is necessary, good, vital to a functioning society, when really all it's doing is making us lazy sacks of shit.

They say the average American human attention span is now 7 seconds. 7 seconds? That's the level of a goldfish. Goldfishologists (or whatever their carnival-science specialty is called) tell us that goldfish, aside from being more orange than gold, live their entire lives in 7 seconds. Whatever they're feeling in that seven seconds, IS their life. They have no concept of the previous 7 and no idea that a future 7 is coming down the stream. They live in the moment, and they have to, otherwise they will get eaten by a bigger fish (and that's most fish since they're small) or get nabbed by opportunistic rigged carnival game providers, whoever supplies carnies with their non-golden goldfish. Honestly, carnie life seems like the better option, but then again, I've never been trapped in a small glass jar while giant drooling morons toss ping-pong balls into a bucket for the right to own me for the week before I die.

And you know what? That's fine for goldfish. Not so much for humans. Whoever directs our distraction (and these days it looks like there are government agencies who do this, and definitely corporate interests) wants us to become modified goldfish. We're not capable of living totally in the moment, most of us aren't doing that anyway, but the evil controllers believe that, through our cell phones, they can keep us so entirely semi-petrified of what might happen in the next 7 seconds that we'll be too preoccupied with hazy, low-level fear to notice how much of money they've stolen and how many of our rights they've stripped.

In the immortal words of Bob Marley, "Get up/Stand up, stand up for your rights"… if you can remember what your rights used to be in the next seven seconds, before we lose focus once again.

KELLY SAYS:

We were a lot more disciplined, that's for sure. If you did something bad outside of the house the older people would see us, they'd discipline us right there, then they'd tell our parents, who would also discipline us. When I first came to the States, in the late 60's, there was still some discipline here. As the years have gone by, that's changed. You can't tell the kids anything these days. We're still a lot more disciplined back home in Jamaica.

What we once called discipline would now be called Child Abuse here. How are you going to have a child and not discipline him? The thing that's gotten lost is how the discipline leads to respect. No kids want to get punished, but they always came back around eventually and appreciated it. We called it being a parent. I don't know what's happening now, but it's not good.

Spare the rod, spoil the child. Yeah, I'm a bit Old Testament, but it doesn't have to be an actual rod, or even a strap, like it was back then in my day. But it has to be something. Maybe take away the damn cell phone for a week. Then the kids could pay attention to what they're doing long enough to actually do it.

I worked farm chores from 4 AM to 8 AM, then went to school from 9-5, then worked in the fields from 6-8 until I was twelve years old. That work ethic sticks with you all your life.

REASON #3 you should SMASH YOUR CELL PHONE:

Kids are losing their grip on what's real and what's not.

The internet is still not THE REAL WORLD, though sadly it's rapidly becoming so. I can't tell you how many times my bank has tried to convince me that online banking is totally safe. You hear news reports of major corporations being hacked, government databases being hacked, but sure, online banking is totally safe. What do they always say is the definition of insanity? Doing the same thing over and over and expecting a different result. Maybe that should be Verizon's new motto – "Keep doing what we tell you, it's got to work out sometime, right?" What about "You're already totally addicted to our product, so just do what we say and buy it, you fucking sheep"? Even if they actually did use that as a corporate slogan, people would still buy their crap. That's how far down the rabbit hole we've sunk.

With the unfortunate advent of Artificial Intelligence, I can't see a future where it's easy to distinguish what's real and what's a damn robot. Do we seriously expect more truth from governments and corporations in the Era of Half Truths? They already lie, now they have the infrastructure to lie to us ALL THE TIME.

As we move more and more aspects of our lives into virtual spaces, we're going to need some sort of Truthometer, some unbiased arbiter of what's real and what's not, but who do we trust enough to make those judgments? It's not the government, not business. It probably should be religious leaders, though their influence has waned a lot in the last few generations. It definitely should be our parents, but the digital divide and the fact that kids are far savvier with technology than their parents sets up some sort of rehashing of the Sixties era slogan “Don’t trust anyone over thirty,” effectively destroying the important aspect of parenting as its always been done, that parents inherently know best. Teenagers eventually realize that’s not true, but if the technology is the medium, and kids know technology better than their parents, then will future parents even have 12-13 years of being always right?

Even our pornography has been invaded by fakitude. OK, admittedly pornography already had fake sex, fake attraction and fake scenarios and a gaggle of fake horny stepmothers, far too willing to have sex with their stepsons, but now it’s half anime, half cartoon, and increasingly A.I. generated. I suppose there is a slight silver lining. A world with fewer regretful aging former female porn stars, while better for the porn stars themselves, is not so good for the masturbators and potentially disastrous for our already tenuous grip on reality.

They've even made sex unreal. And, like thirst or dinner or shelter or childbirth, sex is supposed to be a purely mammalian experience, a weirdly grounding and bonding experience, and so is probably best done without technology. Ironically, we always use new technology for murder and sex first, every time. It's what people do, as would other mammals if they could crack the Opposable Thumb quandary.

Basically, they, the evil and powerful they, are trying to get us to forget how animalistic we are…in order to control even more aspects of our lives. Their conduit for nonsense? That stupid little rectangle you call a cell phone. Smash it! Smash it now. I know the thought scares you, but you WILL feel free afterward. You will BE free.

KELLY SAYS:

I met a lady at Walmart the other day. We got to talking and we wound up talking about cell phones. "Oh, the cell phone has just taken up everything. Even my daughter doesn't communicate with me anymore." That's what she said.

Aren't these things supposed to be for communication? Isn't that why they call them phones?

And now parents are giving them to kids, practically to babies. They distract the kid away from the good things in front of their faces, away from life itself.

We had a solid foundation when I was little.

Even crime is different now. It used to be easier to know who was a criminal and wasn't. I remember once, back in Jamaica, when I was in my twenties, I was married to the daughter of the boss of a painting company. I was running one of the paint crews and there were two ways that a few of my co-workers were stealing from the boss. One was simple. One guy used to bring little empty bags with him and he'd hide and dip the brush in the paint can and then squeeze out paint into the bags, enough to work side paint jobs on his own. Another guy would claim to deliver cash on payday to the guys who didn't show up that day, but he'd pocket it instead. I figured out these schemes and wound up putting an end to them, saving my father-in-law $40,000. I wasn't the most popular guy at work after that. The point is, I figured out these schemes, I knew the players.

Crime now is so computerized that you never even see the guy who's stealing from you, it's all through the computer, the cell phone. Technology pushes us apart.

REASON #4 you should SMASH YOUR CELL PHONE:

They're not only causing mental and emotional problems, but physical ones, too.

If Charles Darwin was correct about evolutionary traits being adaptations to the environment, then isn't it just a matter of time before humans grow gigantic, uber-strong thumbs? Thumbs the size of hot dogs? Thumb wrestling will become a professional sport and people will wear the jerseys of their favorite Thumb Team.

Though these evil little blinking pieces of shit have only really been in wide circulation for about twenty years at the time Kelly and I are writing this, that's still one entire generation, as the sociologists define it, of cell phone addicts. The three major physical areas of concern are eyes, backs and necks.

Our eyesight is getting worse as we spend hours a day in front of the blue light emitted from computers. Once again, it would be tolerable, much more manageable, had they not been shrunk down to fit into pockets. It may be a boon for the optometry industry, but not so good for our collective eyesight. We already don't eat enough vitamin A, now we add the blue light into the mix, then we addict everyone TO the blue light to the extent that they look at it right when they wake up and right before they go to sleep, and you've got an ocular epidemic waiting in the wings.

There's now such widespread acceptance of these evil little things that clothing is now made with cell phone-sized pockets, even on otherwise form-fitting girl clothes. That's America for you. We take a bad idea and then we stretch it out as far as humanly possible, until it barely even resembles its original stupidity.

Our national back health is already rather poor. We hunch. We slouch. We've collectively forgotten the Victorian posture lessons. "Stand up straight, shoulders out, chest forward." It's not only good advice for Eliza Doolittle, it's good advice for everyone, no matter if its aim is to create more prominent cleavage or to keep your spine as taut as possible for your waning years. It's even more important for women than men. While men, unfortunately, develop our own mini-boobs later in life, they're generally not as large or as much of a test for our backs as women's, at least not large enough to necessitate man bras. Ninety-somethings of either gender often develop small but literal hunchbacks, and that helps no one. I bet older Victorian ladies didn't hunch. They, or rather their parents and tutors, had planned out how to prevent it decades earlier. As we collectively bend all the time over to look at our cell phones, don't you think the hunch is going to start coming far earlier now?

This is just one of the many lessons we could, should we be so inclined, learn from the Victorian Era. Don't slouch, train yourself not to slouch. This matters more now that we worship little flashing cellular pocket gods while sitting, standing, walking, lying down, or really any other posture you can imagine. Constantly looking down was once considered a mark of shyness, now it's a mark of cell phonitude (Well, personally I think it's the Mark of the Beast, but I promised I'd try and stick to the chapter subjects). This will have ramifications for our spines. Pocket gods have only been around for twenty years or so, in their current form, so there really hasn't even been enough time for a proper longitudinal study on this, but it's time to start. It will prove me right.

The neck is another area of high concern. Necks are vulnerable places, they need to be stretched, shaken out occasionally and allowed to exercise their full range of motion. It's been a common area for muscle cramps long before cell phones were commonplace, and future human neck health, like so many other areas of modern life, is going to be negatively affected by this constant worshipful pose that people adopt to access the cellular world.

Is it just me or does the way that people tend to view their cell phones remind you of praying? It makes sense, given how much we do, kind of worship them already. Unlike say the Greek or Roman gods, these particular pocket gods aren't offering anything positive for our devotion, and yet we're still idolizing them and, like the ancients, we're routinely making sacrifices to these gods. Instead of a little food and some trinkets, we're sacrificing our sanity, our attention spans and even our own health. You'd think the pocket gods would offer us a little something good in return. Watch a technology-enraptured teenager walking down the sidewalk sometimes, head bent reverentially, eyes downcast, not looking nor caring about the "real world" happening all around them and then try to tell me that they're *not* our gods.

KELLY SAYS:

Give it a few generations and they'll all have giraffe necks and thumbs the size of ears of corn.

REASON #5 you should SMASH YOUR CELL PHONE:

We're losing our privacy and we barely seem to care.

They're tracking devices. By this point, everybody knows this, but it hasn't led to the cell phone smashfest that, in a more rational world, it would have. The cell phone companies track you. The government tracks you through your cell phone. Advertisers pay for the right to eavesdrop on your conversations. That's why, after you spend a few minutes talking about how much you want to buy a boat, a deck chair or some dandruff shampoo, advertisements for boats, deck chairs and dandruff shampoo magically pop up on your screen.

There are some who laud the speed of

their desires being fulfilled. These people have missed half the point of desire itself, working toward something, hunting for the best something, or even being the one in control of the quest for that something. Nothing worth having has ever come as easily as a cell phone pop-up ad, nothing. Nothing. Not a dream job, not a decent marriage, not an experience you'll remember later. Now that it's possible to buy random appliances, vehicles, Eastern European mail-order brides and houses over the internet, we've all but lost the concept of the quest for a thing. It's the journey that defines the quest, not the destination.

It's bad enough that our government is so insecure that it feels the need to blatantly violate the Fourth Amendment, but now corporations are in on the theft, too. For the record, the Fourth Amendment reads:

> *The right of the people to be secure in their persons, houses, papers, and effects, against unreasonable*

searches and seizures, shall not be violated, and no Warrants shall issue, but upon probable cause, supported by Oath or affirmation, and particularly describing the place to be searched, and the persons or things to be seized.

Well, shit, if routine cell phone tracking and unwarranted eavesdropping doesn't violate this Amendment, then what does? It violates almost every word of the Amendment. We're not secure in our houses if someone is listening. We're not secure in our papers (or at least the electronic equivalent) if someone is reading our emails. How is this NOT unreasonable? Also, they're doing it without a Warrant, to everyone, all the time, without in any way describing the place to be searched or the things, or thoughts, or words to be seized. I don't see how this isn't the most blatant violation of this sacred Amendment yet conceived of by man…if you can call the angry, friendless nerds who make these things men.

The pop-up eaves-ad is just sickening to me. Jesus, we already have online stores that sell everything. One particular store named after a popular South American river comes to mind.

To add insult to injury, companies are not only spying on us all the time, but then turning around and selling that data to other companies, so that they too can rape our privacy. Sure, it's not legal mandate that one must own a cell phone, but as the world tries its damndest to move every aspect of our lives online, it's starting to get that way.

Shockingly, my advice for turning this around is the same advice as it was in the last chapter, and the one before and the one before that. Smash the living shit out of your cell phone. It's not your friend. Hell, it's essentially your enemy. And your enemy is charging you forty bucks a month to violate your privacy. Smash it before it's too late.

KELLY SAYS:

It seems pretty crazy to me that no one objects to the cellie phone tracking. Why would anyone want to carry around something that tells the government and the phone company where you are? Why doesn't this bother the cellie phone people? On the farm where I grew up, even though we didn't have the technology back then, we did want to keep track of our animals, otherwise a lot of them would wander off, get killed by predators or get stolen by people. Cattlemen have always branded their cows. Even dog people put collars on them with an address, in case they get lost. Modern farmers low-jack their animals, so they know if the cows wander off into a ditch or the goats have climbed the fence and gotten into the crops. Believe it or not, this isn't bad. It's fine for the animals.

Basically, the kids have become herd animals.

They don’t think for themselves, they eat whatever crap is put before them, they’re stupid and they don’t mind being low-jacked. They look at their cellie phones so much that I’m surprised they aren’t all wandering into ditches, just like cows.

REASON #6 you should SMASH YOUR CELL PHONE:

They're causing major public health issues.

These things really are killing us. Cancer was already rampant, now it looks like it's an inevitable result of using cell phones. Isn't the fear of cancer why we started putting warning labels on cigarette packs?

There are many. According to one of the studies I read for research, cell phones are now used by 97% of American adults. 97%?!? That's more popular than cars, more popular than ice cream, more popular than heroin… also far more addictive and arguably more dangerous. At least heroin addicts know that their lifestyle is killing them. Cell phone users barely question it.

Cell phones transmit their signals through radio frequency radiation (RFR). It says it right there in the third word of the name, radiation. Hold on, isn't radiation bad? Isn't that why only two nuclear bombs have ever been dropped on human populations, and isn't that at least partially because we didn't totally know what would happen back in 1945? Isn't radiation why we limit certain diagnostic medical tests and the nurses wear specialized baseball catcher armor when they administer them? Isn't radiation deadly?

Yes. Yes, it is. And yet…

In the late 2010s, the U.S. Food and Drug Administration (FDA) directed the National Toxicology Program (NTP) to look into radiation risks from specifically 2G and 3G cell phones. As always, it was the white rats who bore the brunt of this research. We must really hate white rats. They're our favorite guinea pigs, more popular than actual guinea pigs for guinea pigging.

Basically, they intermittently exposed rats and mice to RFR for up to two years, beginning in the rat womb and when the mice were a few weeks old, 10 minutes on then 10 minutes off for nine hours each day: 1.5-6 watts per kilogram of body weight for rats and 2.5-10 watts per kilogram in mice (Smith-Roe, Wyde, et al., 2019). I don't know why they preferred the rats to the mice. Granted, 4 and 5G do use different types of signal modulation, but by different I don't mean safer.

The conclusions were EXACTLY what you'd expect. Male rats developed tumors in their hearts, brains and adrenal glands. They couldn't definitely say the female rat tumors were directly from exposure to RFR…but that means they had tumors, too. In fact, lower body weights in newborn rats and their mothers were also observed and nobody wants a skinny baby, even a rat.

Just go ahead and smash your cell phone. When it comes down to a choice between brain tumors and a land line, is that really a choice at all?

KELLY SAYS:

Yep, Bowen's right. I run a restaurant in a college town, so I see a lot of college kids. They all have their little cellie phones. A lot of them look hollow, just shells like their snails crawled away looking for a better home. Not enough sun, not enough exercise, not enough of the stuff that makes people people.

REASON #7 you should SMASH YOUR CELL PHONE:

They're stunting our mental and emotional development.

And let's face it, we were already pretty freaking mentally and emotionally immature. We're the country where fifty-year-old men routinely wear cargo shorts to work and divorced middle-aged women snipe at each other at the grocery store like high school mean girls. We couldn't afford to fall even farther down the immaturity ladder, and yet we have.

Granted, a lot of the evidence of this obvious human decline is due specifically to social media, but where are the teenagers accessing this social media? Why are they able to stay up until 4 AM obsessively checking in with the invisible nonsense? How can they access it on the bus, at a dinner table and pretty much everywhere else? Because of cell phones, of course.

Teenagers were already pretty fucked up before cell phones, but now it's so extreme that I seriously worry about the future of mankind. I know that plopping your kid down in front of a screen does make life temporarily easier for parents, and I sympathize, but it's a short-term fix with far too many negative side effects.

According to a Canadian study (Elia Abi-Jaoude, Karline Treurnicht Naylor and Antonio Pignatiello – great names – Smartphones, social media use and youth mental health, 2020), between 2009 and 2014 admissions to hospitals for self-harm (pre-suicide suicide) increased by 110% in Canadian girls. 110%?!?!!! That's a hell of a lot of depression. Even if this study wasn't clearly about social media use, you'd know that was the culprit, given the time period and the single biggest change in teenagers' lives compared to every other previous group of teens being the ubiquity of cell phones. This has nothing to do with Canadian winters or overuse of maple syrup. In America, between 2011 and 2018, self-poisoning rates for 10-18 year olds increased substantially. Teenagers have always been moody, but now they're literally poisoning themselves thanks to the pocket internet.

And yet, for some reasons passing all understanding, parents still give them to their children. They just *give them* to the kids as presents. I don't get it. I just don't get it.

A lot of this nonsense is clearly a massive outgrowth of what Hollywood has always done to young girls. Comparing themselves to attractive starlets may have helped the hair and skin care industries' bottom lines, and has been a big boon to the SSRI pushers (depression pills), but it's not so helpful for the teenage girls themselves. Now with pocket internet, girls can feel bad about themselves everywhere. It happens with boys too, but to a much smaller extent. The workout bros online are an impossible physical standard to achieve, but more teenage boys possess massive helpings of unearned confidence than teenage girls.

Our medical gurus can't even agree on a definition of Smartphone addiction, even though it's as obvious as the sun rising in the East, even though anyone who has even stood within ten feet of a teenager since 2005 knows they're addicted. Even dogs can see it when you haven't moved for ten minutes and they're still standing right on top of their poop. Even so, we can't even agree that they're addictive, even when they're designed to promote addiction, we still can't agree. I don't know if this is because of industry-funded studies, too much political power for "communication" companies or if it's just the fart on our collective elevator that we smell but don't want to acknowledge. No matter the reason, it's true.

An analysis of US annual data showed an exposure-response relationship between electronically addled adolescents who stare zombie-like into their rectangles for more than 2 hours a day and insufficient sleep. Teenagers need more shut eye than adults, they're still developing. Instead of sleeping, they're consulting a little rectangle that makes them feel bad about themselves and causes them to cut themselves and consider suicide. If it weren't real, if it weren't everywhere, it'd just be crazy.

ADHD, poor academic performance, cognitive developmental delays, and less sleep. These are some of the big ones. However, since most existing studies are cross-sectional, we've barely even begun to admit, much less fully document, the harm these little pieces of evil are causing. One sure-fire cure is smashing the hell of out of cell phone.

KELLY SAYS:

I'm a busy man, I'm not going to comment on any more of these chapter topics. Do you not get it by now? Cell phones are bad. I hate them, and you should, too.

Bowen's right, just smash them, look up at the sun, take a deep breath and go live your life the right way, the way God intended. You'll be a lot happier, more productive and more intelligent.

That's it. You know where I stand, I'm done even thinking about this craziness.

REASON #8 you should SMASH YOUR CELL PHONE:

They're changing our sense of manners.

Let's hope this one doesn't stick, but I'm not optimistic. Think about it. It was only twenty-five years ago that taking a phone call when you were previously engaged in face-to-face conversation would've been considered the height of rudeness. To prioritize the invisible person over the living human in front of you **is** quite rude, but now commonplace.

Even if mobile phones had existed in the mid-twentieth century, they probably would've been de-prioritized, in favor of the human being in front of you, whether that human was your spouse, your therapist or even the girl at the check-out line at Publix.

It still would've been considered ill-mannered to talk on the phone instead of living in the moment, taking care of what's in front of you.

The sense of self-importance that cell phones have given people is immense, and rather silly. America has always promoted the idea that being busy means that you matter more, but even under that somewhat ridiculous logic, does having your mother call you while you're at the beauty salon mean that you're somehow important? Unless the Pope is calling, then no, you're not important. And even if it IS the Pope, you should tell him you'll call him back after you take care of what's right in front of you. It's the decent thing to do.

Cell phones have decimated the doorbell, eliminating yet another task from the average butler's daily routine. My god, they're destroying butlers. What will older, distinguished, obsequious Englishmen do for a living now?

What cell phones have done to the family dinner is unforgivable. It was already hard enough to get your kids to talk and share the events of their day over a sensible meal and not rush off to do teenage things, even before the introduction of beeping nonsense flashing boxes into the equation. Granted, smart parents will still, even now, make their kids turn them off during dinner, but that can only happen if the parents aren't also caught up in the phone-craziness, and how many modern parents can make that claim? This is the world's biggest and most dangerous addiction, and it knows no age boundaries. The family dinner used to mean something. Lives were shared over food. Lessons were learned, jokes were told and emotions were shared. They framed family life in a way that cheap delivered artery-crushing fast food, ordered via cell phone and eaten in silence while everyone consults his pocket god, can never do.

Finally, after twenty years of cell phonitude, schools have realized that letting students carry these things to class is just asking for mass dumbassery. It's hard to believe that it took two decades, but it did. At the very least, students should have to exercise a small degree of creativity in their never-ending quest for mischief. That way they could at least learn something useful. Learning how to get away with stuff in life is a skill that comes in handy later on.

REASON #9 you should SMASH YOUR CELL PHONE:

It's decimating creativity, just stabbing creativity through the heart, while we watch it slowly bleed out on the floor.

As any artistic person will tell you, creativity begins with boredom. That's the origin of artistry…not having enough childhood friends. Along with the equally-creativity-murdering suburban habit of over-scheduling and over-protecting our kids, we've added the cell phone, as the final shock of the electric chair to the death sentence we proscribed for future artistry.

The government loves this. Creative people make more trouble, don't blindly follow rules and tend to question the logic of what they're told. Governments don't want to be questioned, they want to be obeyed. Business pretty much works this way, too. What passes for creativity these days pales in comparison to the past, when childhood boredom lead us somewhere positive.

It's hard to tell if this particular reason for smashing your cell phone was on purpose or inadvertent. Either way, the result is the same.

Boredom leads to imagination, imagination leads to story telling, story telling leads to art. Putting flashing neon lights in front of your three-year-old is going to stop any future creativity in its tracks. Much like flying insects, humans are naturally attracted to flashing lights. I'm not sure we can help ourselves any more than dive-bombing kamikaze bugs from running headlong toward flashing lights. Why do you think restaurants put neon OPEN signs in their windows? A wooden or plastic sign could accomplish the same task, letting passersby know that they can enter, but it doesn't attract the eye like lights.

When I was a child, I watched some cartoons, specifically on Saturday mornings, but my mother limited the amount of screen time I had in traditional motherly fashion. "You can have an hour of cartoons, so pick the ones that really matter." Do you know how much more difficult it is to control children's viewing habits when you give them eternal, unlimited access to the device itself? And putting these kiddie-amphetamine devices in cars and in schools is just hammering the final nails into the coffin of what was once a pretty creative country.

Creativity isn't only important for artists. Obviously it's the essence of art, but the idea of creativity matters in most other professions and other areas of life as well. Hasn't, say, the automotive industry, flourished when a cool, creative new car design comes out? Think tail fins, hybrid cars, converting surplus military vehicles into road-worthy transportation, cup holders, Lord knows seat belts (and, to a lesser extent, airbags), eye-catching rim designs, hydraulics, "the way back" in station wagons, the 8-Track player and its modern counterparts. These are all creative ideas that we now take for granted in cars, but when they first arrived, they were creative and interesting.

And that's just one business example. If we had more creative people in government, we might not have half the problems we now have. If we had more creative people in academia, we might have a better informed populace (I felt a little bad about that one because the best teachers are creative, but how many great teachers do most U.S. public school students get in 12 years? A handful? Five at most?).

Dovetailing the end of creativity with the rise of Artificial Intelligence feels pre-planned to me. I have no data to back that up, but the timing feels a little suspect, given that A.I. is primed not so much to enhance our creativity as to replace it. Since the current large language model of A.I. is inherently a race to the middle (averaging the sum of knowledge and reverting it to the mean), we're going to have to work hard to hold onto what little ingenuity, what precious small amount of creativity we have left.

REASON #10 you should SMASH YOUR CELL PHONE:

Attempting to fit simply *<u>everything</u>* *into this one little device is a recipe for control and inherently unsafe.*

They're really trying hard to fit as many aspects of our lives as possible onto cell phones. Consider the vast array of services they offer: dating, sending work documents, banking, medicine, verbal communication, written communication, video chatting, e-books and audio books, ironic zen-inducing calm nature scenes and/or nature sounds (trying to calm yourself through cell phones is tin-foil underwear insane), ordering dinner, ordering airplane tickets, ordering therapy, ordering hookers (at least in Nevada), finding a job, losing a job, job-related memos, pay-ing for pretty much everything, the news (if you can even still call it that), genealogy, and a steady never-ending camera trained on your house pets so you can watch what they do when you're not home. And those are just the ones I could think of off the top of my head.

The current and future problems this can, does and will cause are immense. First off, if everything is done through these evil little rectangles, what do you do when you lose it or it gets stolen? Unlike, say, a stolen credit card, you can't just cancel everything in your life, and since you would normally communicate with everything through your little everything device, how would you even go about canceling it all?

Secondly, I'm not sold on these things being particularly secure. The government's access to your most personal information is made easier with cell phone, but that's only the tip of the iceberg of crazy here. Unlike pre-internet thieves, hackers can break into computer systems from anywhere in the world. How does that make preventing, or Lord knows, solving crime any easier? Can't a decent twelve-year-old hacker cover his tracks? He practically lives in a virtual world, I'm guessing he learned how to throw the authorities off his scent at age six.

We hear about massive computer hacks all the time now, but we're still not questioning the logic of online banking? I don't care how much security we build into the rectangles, the criminals are going to find a way around it. It feels like a scammy arms race between the pure thieves and the cell phone companies, who are just more accepted, better dressed thieves themselves. The only losers in this race? Us, the people. EVERYONE.

Doesn't putting everything onto the flashing rectangles which people check in with every few minutes pretty much mean that these things are now our best friends? Hell, they're more than that. They're our best friends, our financial advisors, our general practitioners, our religious leaders, our teachers, our mothers, our navigators, our therapists, our entertainers and, probably soon, our lovers. Essentially, they're our gods. No wonder we assume a worshipful pose when looking at them.

REASON #11 you should SMASH YOUR CELL PHONE:

Their basic promises are complete lies.

What do cell phones promise? They promise connectivity. They promise access to a world of information. They promise safety. They promise convenience. For today's teenagers, they essentially promise adulthood.

Because of them, we're less connected, on any real level that matters, than we were when we had land lines, and far less connected than we were in a time before telephones existed. When communication had to be done through the mail, or better yet face-to-face, people had longer, deeper conversation. They had to, not knowing when they might see far-flung friends and relatives again.

Read a Colonial-era letter sometime. Read a Renaissance-era letter. Read any letter written before there were more convenient alternatives to writing a letter. You'll discover poetry, transmission of profound ideas, real experiences, hopes, dreams, fears, cursive curlicues that inspire awe, lengthy updates about the lives of loved ones. You'll discover communication, what human communication once was before we lost our attention spans and forgot how to communicate.

Yes, it is undoubtedly easier and faster to communicate now. There is no denying that, but this ease has led to shorthand, an onslaught of internetish acronyms posing as words. Worse yet, it's led us to use smiley faces in adult communication. Smiley faces (now known as emojis because compu-laziness has let tech people rename old stuff and make us think it's new) used to be reserved for teenage girls' diaries and motherly love notes to six-year-olds. Now they inhabit corporate memos and text messages between ninety-year-olds. Their very speed and ease have weakened the language to the point that I'm worried that, if we continue this trend much longer, we're all going to be grunting like cavemen. I wonder what the grunt emojis are going to look like.

The world of information that is the internet isn't entirely a lie…just most of it. There is some true wisdom online, but for the most part, the internet, and worse still the handheld internet, has more blatant lies, fear-mongering and manipulation than a tabloid newspaper written by lunatics bent on taking over the world. In fact, I blame lunatics bent on taking over the world. They're more often called tech billionaires and the politicians they own, but they're still power-starved crazy people. If they didn't have so damn much money and influence, we might not all be trapped in their fear-porn world of half truths and constant anger/arousal. So, yes, cell phones do, theoretically, give people a pathway to mountains of information, but since most of it is utter crap, how is this helping us?

For reasons passing all understanding, today's parents think that giving their children cell phones is going to make their lives safer. Granted, it does make it easier to call them or for them to call you, but haven't teenagers always mainly called their parents when they need money? Sure, I'll admit that calling a new-age taxi is safer than driving home drunk, but drunk driving still happens, and driving drunk was a poor choice even before the advent of the cell phone, and taxis aren't new, just rebranded and cell phonized.

And, while I'm admitting the lame arguments for the other side of this equation do have some slight merit, I must admit that, though it's bizarre and not helpful for the psyche of modern teenagers, the tracking of your children through cell phones probably does provide some level of safety…but it's 100% not worth it. Not only is it extremely creepy that parents are low-jacking their children, it only contributes to the modern plague of protracted adolescence sweeping our nation. The underlying emotion of cellular technology was supposed to be hope. That's what they all promised, hope, a better, more connected world, like Star Trek. Instead, they've given us fear and suspicion. They promised us Jean Luc Picard and instead we got The Borg.

Yes, their promise of convenience is real. You can order food to your door anywhere in the country now. Before, with the exception of pizza, that was only true in New York City. You can watch movies on city buses. You can do your taxes, renew your insurance and pay your bills from the palm of your hand. The promise of convenience is real. Unfortunately, this convenience has only exacerbated humanity's worst instincts. We're eating even shittier food, we're watching far more and far worse porn, we've reduced dating to an algorithm, and made applying for jobs as inhuman as humanly possible. The convenience is real, but that was the <u>last</u> thing humanity needed.

As I said earlier, cell phones promise adulthood. Much like the automobile, they've become a symbol for American maturity, and yes, that, too, is a giant lie. If eighteen-year-olds were discussing Plato and Nietzsche via text message, or pondering what diet and exercise routine would lead to fewer doctor visits, hashing out international differences to put an end to war or even making decent jokes, and giving money to the poor, then the cell phone liars might have a point. A few generations back only adolescents wore cargo shorts to work and a few generations before *that*, there was no such thing as adolescence. You were a kid, then you aged out of it and you were an adult. Now we just remain children until we, ourselves, have kids. That still forces you into adulthood, or at least the veneer of maturity. But that would be true even in a world of fax machines and telegraph operators.

Almost everything cell phones promise is a lie, except the few that aren't, but even the few honest promises of the technology are only making people dumber, angrier, less informed and anxious about everything under the sun.

REASON #12 you should SMASH YOUR CELL PHONE:

Modern slavery is heavily involved in their creation.

Multinational corporations have done an extremely effective job of hiding it, but modern slavery is, indeed, involved in the mining of cobalt and other digital building blocks, other necessary ingredients for the creation of cellular telephones. Read the outstanding investigative journalism book *Cobalt Red* by Siddarth Kara. He does a better job of explaining this chain of evil than I ever could.

OK, it's not technically slavery in the sense that the "workers" could, theoretically, quit and work a different job. However, practically-speaking, these workers have no other choice. Where else could they find work that pays them enough to feed their families? The conditions are as bad if not worse than actual slave cabins. The treatment of the workers? Well, let's just say OSHA would have a coronary. These mines are mainly in central Africa, so while US standards aren't applied, the gigantic profits are going to American and Chinese companies, so shouldn't the standards be the same?

Is this level of hypocrisy sustainable? Clearly, I'm not a fan of the current teenage generation's telephonic habits, but in their defense they do have a keen nose for oppression. How they would react to modern slavery is anyone's guess, because after reading about the lengths the mine operators reached in trying to keep all relevant information away from Kara, the parallels to American slave narratives of the Old South were hard to ignore: disease, no means of recourse, no limits on cruelty and no regard for the miners as fellow human beings. To be fair, more of the blame should land on Chinese companies (and the CCP, since authoritarian societies bind government and business – if that feels familiar, just wait a few years) than on American ones…but we still deserve plenty of blame.

The thing is, we don't all need to participate in this exercise of willful ignorance. Even in a world awash in cell phones, we could do it humanely. Of course, I'd prefer a world with no cell phones whatsoever. Land lines didn't require any slavery at all.

America has always had a hard time living up to our ideals. Difficulty practicing what we preach has always been an American issue. Ask any foreigner pretty much anywhere else in the world, and you'll see what I mean. Our news of the world outside our borders is so sparse and terribly uninformative that few of us notice the raging hypocrisy, but I have some faith that Gen Alpha (or whatever ridiculous name we're now calling the kids' generation – come on, Gen Alpha sounds like Cain and Abel's generation) may see through this particular smokescreen. For all of their faults, they are laser-focused on mass oppression, and this surely qualifies. Unfortunately, they're also wildly addicted to their cell phones, so, honestly, it's a toss up.

I propose that it should be a "toss down," as in toss your smartphone onto the ground and smash it, with a shoe, a stone, a giant dictionary, a brick, a concrete block, a gym weight of 30 lbs or more, a microwave oven, a steel beam, an iron rod, a bal peen hammer, a sledgehammer, a jackhammer, really any type of hammer, or basically anything heavy enough for proper smashing. I'd recommend running them over with a car or, better yet, tying them to railroad tracks (as a nod to the penny-smashing of yore), but it's more emotionally satisfying the closer you are to the physical smashing, the more control you have in the cell phone smashing process.

DATA:

In his groundbreaking and outstanding book *The Anxious Generation*, social scientist Jonathan Haidt warned us about the dangers of the electronically-based childhoods of the generations of children who have grown up in this age of runaway technology, epitomized by the cell phone. He compared every single previous generation's upbringing to the last two, and his verdict was clear. A play-based childhood is better than a tech-based one. Because the effect of technology, more than any other legacy, is fear, fear, and more fear. We read about an earthquake on the other side of the planet, and then we worry about earthquakes. We learn about a school shooting and assume that they're going to happen at our kids' school in the next few weeks. There's an amplifying effect to the internet, and what it amplifies more than anything else is FEAR.

So that this isn't entirely just my voice, I thought I'd include links to a couple of studies you could read to back up what I've said and what you already suspect. You could type these into a computer and look them up, or you could wallow in irony and point a cell phone at them, take a picture and then link… which may be faster but the irony of doing *that* for *this* book may weigh you down so much that you bust through asphalt, sink into pavement and cause minor earthquakes, merely from the weight of all that irony. But as long as that's the last time you use your cell phone before smashing the living shit out of it, then it'll be a great final use and the first day of the rest of your free life.

Here are just a few research studies (mainly so you don't think this book is just a bunch of angry rants that sounds vaguely like your grandfather yelling at joggers or house pets):

https://theconversation.com/how-technology-is-reshaping-childrens-development-the-good-the-bad-and-the-unknown-268148

This article from a website called The Conversation shares some insights from several journals and studies.

https://www.researchgate.net/publication/403245614_Children_Cell_Phones_and_Reading_Comprehension

This one generally agrees with me that cell phones are bad, especially for kids. Though it does differentiate between English-speaking households and Spanish-speaking ones, saying only the English speakers suffered in reading comprehension. I have a theory that that result is about learning a second language and how the learning trumps the negative effects...because learning is good. And while cell phones pretend to teach, they mainly slowly suck the marrow of your soul like the world's nerdiest vampire, bit by bit, over time, until you're left as a shell of a human, blindly repeating nonsensical opinions spat out online, with no sense of creativity and original thought, with the ultimate goal of creating a population of brain-dead morons bumping into each other at the supermarket and starting fights (because remember, cell phones also teach rudeness and kill manners and empathy) over minor inconveniences… not that I have any strong feelings on the matter.

https://www.reviews.org/mobile/cell-phone-addiction/

This recent study on American cell phone habits has plenty of statistics for the number-lovers. Here's some of the most relevant:

> How often do people check their phones every day? Though the average has dropped below last year's numbers, Americans still check their phones nearly 200 times a day – or about once every five minutes while they're awake.

But, in an almost 3% rise from last year, nearly 46% of Americans consider themselves "addicted" to their phones in 2026. It's worth noting that this stat came after a considerable decrease from prior years, possibly due to shaking off pandemic-era habits. Still, it shouldn't be too surprising to hear that 53% say they have never gone more than 24 hours without their phone.

- **Americans check their phones 186 times per day (11.6 times per hour)**
- 72.2% use their phone at work
- 87.4% use their phone while watching TV
- 56.4% use their phone while eating dinner
- 67.9% use their phone on the toilet
- 60.7% have texted someone in the same room
- 49.6% sleep with their phone at night
- 41.3% feel panic/anxiety at <20% battery
- 84.6% check their phone within 10 minutes of waking

The statistic that freaked me out is that last one, almost 85% of people check their phones within 10 minutes of waking up. It's the first thing they do. Not stretching. Not yawning. Not even farting. Besides that obviously being an addiction, it's killed the whole "Embrace the day" philosophy of optimists, since very rarely does the internet provide non-cat-video optimism.

German researchers, publishing in *Computers in Human Behavior*, say three days of abandoning cell phone use rests the brain back to its earlier attention span. Three days, that's all it takes. Most road trips take longer than that, most high-end medical procedures, honeymoons, corporate and/or spiritual retreats. Most summer camps take longer than that. It's that easy. Just put the fucking thing down for 72 hours...then, hopefully, 72 more, etc.

Things change back. Especially the reward centers of the brain and impulse control. Decision-making, focus and gratification all improve with just a three day hiatus. Imagine how much better that could be with just one cathartic smashing.

This German study builds on research by Ken Strayer, a cognitive psychologist at the University of Utah, who basically said the same thing but added "time in nature" into the mix.

There's hope. Smash the living shit out of your cell phone, go roll around in the grass and give it a few days…and then you're free.

No one was afraid of rotary phones. No one was afraid of radio (other than Orson Welles' War of the Worlds, and that seems pretty quaint now, doesn't it?). No one was afraid of giant 1980's car phones, though maybe they should've been.

Something changed around 2004…and not for the better.

The good news is that, despite what you think and what your phone is telling you, no one actually *needs* a cell phone. Deep down, everyone knows these things aren't helping them. That's why, when people learn that I don't own one, they inevitably try to talk me into buying one. The same goes for Kelly. It's not generosity, it's not to get me to join the modern world, it's misery loving company. They know. They know all too well. And a small part of them hates themselves for their addiction.

Smash away, my friends! Everything's better without invisible handcuffs.

www.ingramcontent.com/pod-product-compliance
Lightning Source LLC
LaVergne TN
LVHW050938210926
848482LV00013B/661
* 9 7 9 8 9 9 9 7 8 9 9 0 7 *